Sojourner Truth

by Elizabeth Dana Jaffe

Compass Point Early Biographies

Content Adviser: Professor Sherry L. Field,
Department of Social Science Education, College of Education,
The University of Georgia

Reading Adviser: Dr. Linda D. Labbo,
Department of Reading Education, College of Education,
The University of Georgia

COMPASS POINT BOOKS

Minneapolis, Minnesota

Compass Point Books
3722 West 50th Street, #115
Minneapolis, MN 55410

Visit Compass Point Books on the Internet at *www.compasspointbooks.com* or e-mail your
request to *custserv@compasspointbooks.com*

Photographs ©:
Archive Photos, cover, 6, 8, 10, 20; Visual Language, cover; Battle Creek Historical Society, 4, 7, 11, 14, 16, 17, 18
(left and right), 19 (top and bottom), 22–23, 25; Stock Montage, 9; Schomburg Center for Research in Black Culture,
New York Public Library, 12; Historic VU/Visuals Unlimited, 15; Library of Congress, 21, 24; Scott Michaels, 26.

Editors: E. Russell Primm and Emily J. Dolbear
Photo Researcher: Svetlana Zhurkina
Photo Selector: Linda S. Koutris
Designer: Bradfordesign, Inc.

Library of Congress Cataloging-in-Publication Data

Jaffe, Elizabeth D.
    Sojourner Truth / by Elizabeth D. Jaffe.
        p. cm. — (Compass Point early biographies)
    Includes bibliographical references and index.
    ISBN 0-7565-0068-0
        1. Truth, Sojourner, d. 1883—Juvenile literature. 2. Afro-American abolitionists—Biography—
Juvenile literature. 3. Afro-American women—Biography—Juvenile literature. 4. Abolitionists—
United States—Biography—Juvenile literature. 5. Social reformers—United States—Biography—
Juvenile literature. [1. Truth, Sojourner, d. 1883. 2. Abolitionists. 3. Reformers. 4. Afro-Americans—
Biography. 5. Women—Biography.] I. Title. II. Series.
    E457.905 .R25 2000
    973.7'092—dc21   00-008635

Table of Contents

Born a Slave

Isabella was born a slave. Her family called her Belle. Slaves did not have last names. Belle was probably born sometime in 1797 in Ulster County, New York.

A farmer named Colonel Hardenbergh owned her family. He was a Dutchman, so Belle spoke only Dutch.

Belle was the youngest of nine children. Seven of the children had been sold to other masters. Only Belle and her brother had not yet been sold. But they would be. Belle's mother prepared her for this day.

◀ Sojourner Truth

Taken from Her Family

The time came. Belle was sold at an **auction** when she was eleven. She and her brother were sold to different masters.

Belle's new master was John Nealy. He and his wife spoke English. Belle could not

understand them. The master's wife beat Belle to make her speak English. "I can't understand it, Lord," Belle said. "Is it right for them to hit me when I work so hard?" Soon she learned to speak English with a Dutch accent.

Sojourner Truth was sold at an auction along with a number of sheep.

◀ Daily life was hard for slaves.

Sold Again

Belle was then sold two more times. In 1809, she was sold to the Schryvers. In 1810, she was sold to John Dumont, a New York farmer. Dumont felt very lucky to have Belle.

Slave children were often sold at auctions.

She was a very hard worker. Belle was tall and strong. She worked in the field and cleaned the house.

Fieldwork required great strength.

Forced to Marry

Belle stayed at the Dumonts' farm for seventeen years. She felt very lonely. Her mother and father had died. All her brothers and sisters had been sold.

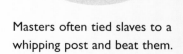

Soon she met Bob. He was a slave on a neighboring farm. They fell in love. Bob's owner was not happy about this. He beat Bob. Belle never saw Bob again.

Masters often tied slaves to a whipping post and beat them.

Belle was forced to marry Thomas, an older slave. Dumont owned Thomas too. In 1815, Belle's first child, Diana, was born. Belle had four other children: Elizabeth, Hannah, Peter, and Sophie.

Like her mother, Belle never knew when one of her children would be sold. She tried to prepare them for this. She taught them to trust in God.

A picture of Diana Corbin (Belle's first child) in old age

Escape to Freedom

In 1817, New York passed a law that freed some slaves. Most would be freed by 1828.

Dumont told Belle he would free her a year early if she promised to work extra hard. Belle promised. But Dumont didn't free her. He said she had not worked hard enough. So Belle decided to escape. She said, "I'll be a slave no more."

A Difficult Decision

Belle wanted her family to stay together. But she felt she had to leave. Belle escaped with baby Sophie. The Van Wageners, a **Quaker** family, helped Belle. They took her into their home.

But Dumont found Belle. He tried to force her back to his farm. The Van Wageners paid Dumont so that they could keep her. The Van Wageners freed Belle and Sophie right away. Belle chose to work for them.

◄ Slaves tried to escape to the
North where they would be free.

Belle Wins in Court

Then Belle found out that Dumont had sold Peter, her five-year-old son. Peter was going to a master in Alabama. This was against the law. Slaves could not be sold to people in a different state. Belle was both angry and sad. Her deep feelings surprised Dumont. He didn't believe slaves had feelings.

Belle went to court to get her son Peter back.

Belle went to a judge to get her son back. The chances of a black woman winning in court were small. But the judge got Peter back. This case was important. A black woman had won.

14

Belle moved to New York City ➤ to live with her son Peter.

New York City

Belle decided to move to New York City with Peter. She felt this would be good for him. Belle left Sophie and her other daughters at the Van Wageners. She found a job as a housekeeper in New York City.

Belle became involved in religious groups. She lived in a community called the **Kingdom**. She also helped home-less women.

These were hard years for Peter. He was always in trouble. When he grew up, he became a sailor. He wrote to his mother. Belle could not read or write but her friends read Peter's letters to her. The letters stopped in 1841. She never heard from Peter again. Belle grew tired of the city and decided to leave.

Belle became a speaker for many religious groups, including the Quakers.

A New Name

Slaves still had no rights. Belle knew that women had no rights either. Many people in the North spoke out against slavery and stood up for women's rights. Belle decided to join them and become a speaker too.

Belle spoke out about freeing slaves.

She changed her name to Sojourner Truth. A **sojourner** is a person who travels from place to place. She chose Truth because she would always tell the truth. Sojourner was clever and very funny. She became a powerful and well-known speaker.

17

A Writer and Speaker

In 1850, a writer named Olive Gilbert told Sojourner's story in a book. It was called *The Narrative of Sojourner Truth*. Sojourner sold the book to help support herself and her travels. She spoke at many meetings. She spoke at women's rights meetings. She told her listeners to demand their rights, not just talk about them.

Truth never learned to read or write. This is the only sample of her handwriting.

Truth's book *The Narrative of Sojourner Truth*

At one of the
meetings, men
said women
were too weak
to be equal.
Sojourner showed them
her strong arms. She said

Downtown Battle Creek
in the early 1860s

she worked as hard as any man. Then she said,
"Aren't I a woman?"

Sometimes Sojourner's life was in danger.
Many people disagreed with her. These people
believed in slavery. They were also against
rights for women.

Sojourner also spoke
at the Seventh-Day
Adventist tabernacle.

The American Civil War

Frederick Douglass was a powerful speaker against slavery. He believed war was the only way to end slavery. Sojourner hoped slavery would end with the help of God.

Frederick Douglass

But, in 1861, the **Civil War** between the Northern and the Southern states began. The people in the North fought against slavery. The people in the South needed slaves to work on their large **plantations**.

20

President Abraham Lincoln signed the **Emancipation Proclamation** in 1863. This proclamation freed the slaves.

Sojourner was thrilled! The hard work of Sojourner and others like her would end in victory.

The Emancipation Proclamation

A Move to Michigan

The bloody and tragic war continued. Many soldiers fought and died in battle after battle.

Sojourner was now living in Battle Creek, Michigan. All her daughters had married and moved there too. Sojourner especially loved her grandson, Sammy Banks.

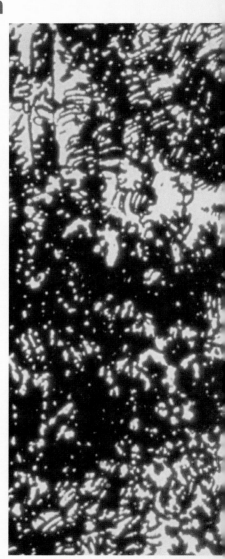

Sojourner Truth lived in this house in Battle Creek, Michigan.

For Aunty
Sojourner Truth

A. Lincoln

Oct. 29. 1864

President Lincoln signed Truth's *Book of Life*.

In 1864, she and Sammy went to
Washington, D.C. There she met President
Abraham Lincoln. He signed Sojourner's
Book of Life, "For Aunty Sojourner Truth,
October 29, 1864."

◄ President Abraham Lincoln and Sojourner Truth

After Freedom

In 1865, the North won the Civil War. The slaves were free at last. The North and South were at peace again. Sojourner stayed in Washington. She ran the Freedmen's Hospital. The hospital took care of sick **freedmen**. Sojourner did everything she could to help freed slaves.

By the 1860s, Sojourner felt too tired and old to travel. She returned to Battle Creek. There she lived happily with her family and friends until her death in 1883.

◀ Sojourner Truth's grave

Important Dates in Sojourner Truth's Life

1797 ?	Isabella is born into slavery in Ulster County, New York
1800	Is sold to Colonel Charles Hardenbergh
1808	Is sold to John Nealy
1809	Is sold to Martin Schryver; Isabella's mother and father die
1810	Is sold again, to John Dumont
1814	Marries a fellow slave named Thomas
1826	Is sold to the Van Wageners, a Quaker family, and is set free
1828	Moves to New York City with son Peter
1843	Changes name to Sojourner Truth
1850	Publishes *The Narrative of Sojourner Truth*
1857	Moves to Battle Creek, Michigan
1865	Works in the Freedmen's Hospital
1883	Dies in Battle Creek, Michigan, on November 26

Glossary

auction—a sale where people bid on things

Civil War—the war between the Northern and Southern states that lasted from 1861 to 1865. The North wanted to keep the states together and ban slavery. The South wanted to be separate and keep slavery. The North won.

Emancipation Proclamation—a document signed on January 1, 1863, by Lincoln that freed slaves in the South

freedmen—freed slaves

Kingdom—a religious community

plantation—a large farm where crops such as cotton were grown

Quaker—a religious group that is against slavery and war

sojourner—a person who travels from place to place

Did You Know?

- Sojourner didn't know when her birthday was. Her master, Colonel Hardenbergh, might have written it down with his farm animals' birth records. These records were either thrown away or lost.

- Sojourner worked hard for John Dumont. Sometimes she worked all night to finish her tasks.

- Sojourner tried, unsuccessfully, to have land in the West given to freedmen.

Want to Know More?

At the Library

Ferris, Jeri. *Walking the Road to Freedom: A Story about Sojourner Truth.* Minneapolis: Carolrhoda, 1988.

Krass, Peter. *Sojourner Truth.* New York: Chelsea House Publishers, 1988.

McKissack, Patricia, and Fredrick McKissack. *Sojourner Truth: Ain't I a Woman?* New York: Scholastic, Inc., 1992.

On the Web

The Sojourner Truth Institute

http://www.sojournertruth.org

For a look at Sojourner Truth's life and work

Through the Mail

The Sojourner Truth Institute of Battle Creek

5 Riverwalk Center

34 West Jackson Street

Battle Creek, MI 49017

To get information about Sojourner Truth and her life in Battle Creek

On the Road

Historical Society of Battle Creek

Battle Creek, MI 49017

616/965-2613

To see the most complete collection of things related to Sojourner Truth

Index

About the Author
Elizabeth Dana Jaffe lives in New York City. After graduating from Brown University, she received her master's degree in early education from and taught at Bankstreet College in New York City. Since then, Elizabeth has written and edited educational materials. Elizabeth Dana Jaffe respects the never-ending fight and gentle strength of Sojourner Truth.